Scarves & Cowls

Reflect your personal style with scarves and cowls in custom widths and lengths! Complete instructions are given for the 12 projects shown inside. Plus, easy-to-follow charts are your guide to dozens more sizes. The options are endless!

4

8

12

16

20

24

LEISURE ARTS, INC.
Maumelle, Arkansas

MEET THE DESIGNER
Karen Ratto-Whooley

Karen Ratto-Whooley says childhood crochet lessons from her Italian grandmother helped her become the designer that she is today. "She didn't speak English, so she didn't know how to read an American pattern," Karen explains. "She taught me how to 'read the pictures' in order to create the item in the book. Because of this, I tended to make patterns differently than they were written, because many times I had to figure out how it was put together. So technically I consider myself a designer from the age of 7!"

Karen's designs for knitting, crochet, and the Knook have been published in numerous books and magazines, and she teaches nationwide at special events and in classes at guilds and yarn shops. A self-described "computer geek at heart," she does her own web design and marketing for her indie pattern line, KRW Knitwear Studio.

For more about Karen, visit her website, www.KRWknitwear.com.

How to Use This Book

Each of the six designs in this book is shown in two sizes, as a scarf and a cowl. Complete instructions are provided for making the photographed models, so you don't have to change a thing to come out with wonderful results.

To give you more options, we've already done the math for numerous sizes of each design. Easy-to-follow charts list the measurements for each size, the skeins of yarn needed, and the stitch count for the beginning chain.

On the facing page, you can see our two variations of the Mary design on pages 4-7. Notice how the same pattern and yarn has been used to produce a 4" wide scarf and a 13½" tall cowl.

Besides varying the sizes, you also can change up the look of each design with your yarn choice. Look for different textures, choose between solid versus variegated colors, or pick novelty yarns with special effects such as sequins.

Six designs, with 8 sizes for each scarf and 8 sizes for each cowl, gives you a total of 96 pre-planned variations in this book. Just in case you still don't find the size you want, we've also provided instructions for how to calculate larger or smaller sizes, using the pattern Multiple (see page 30).

Creating a scarf or cowl that is exactly what you want has never been easier. Just imagine all of the possibilities!

WE'VE DONE THE MATH FOR YOU!

Just choose the size you want from our easy-to-follow charts, such as these examples of the Mary design from pages 4-7.

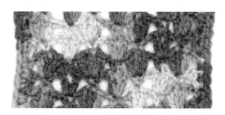

Size (inches)	Size (centimeters)	Skein(s) needed	Beginning chain
4 x 60	10 x 152.5	2	26

Size (inches)	Size (centimeters)	Skein(s) needed	Beginning chain
13½ x 40	34.5 x 101.5	3	86

CUSTOMIZE YOUR SCARF

The beginning chain for this pattern is a multiple of 6 + 2 *(see Multiples, page 30)*. Choose a size below, work the beginning chain, then follow the instructions until the Scarf measures the desired length. The yarn needed for each size is based on getting the specified gauge with a Super Fine Weight yarn with 230 yards (210 meters) per skein.

Size (inches)	Size (centimeters)	Skein(s) needed	Beginning chain
4 x 40	10 x 101.5	1	26
4 x 54	10 x 137	1	26
4 x 60	10 x 152.5	2	26
6 x 40	15 x 101.5	2	38
6 x 54	15 x 137	2	38
6 x 60	15 x 152.5	2	38
9¾ x 40	25 x 101.5	2	62
9¾ x 54	25 x 137	3	62

CUSTOMIZE YOUR COWL

The beginning chain for this pattern is a multiple of 6 + 2 *(see Multiples, page 30)*. Choose a size below, work the beginning chain, then follow the instructions until the Cowl measures the desired circumference. The yarn needed for each size is based on getting the specified gauge with a Super Fine Weight yarn with 230 yards (210 meters) per skein.

Size (inches)	Size (centimeters)	Skein(s) needed	Beginning chain
4 x 28	10 x 71	1	26
4 x 40	10 x 101.5	1	26
6 x 28	15 x 71	1	38
6 x 40	15 x 101.5	2	38
9¾ x 28	25 x 71	2	62
9¾ x 40	25 x 101.5	2	62
13½ x 28	34.5 x 71	2	86
13½ x 40	34.5 x 101.5	3	86

MARY

 **EASY**

SHOPPING LIST

Yarn (Super Fine Weight)

[1.76 ounces, 230 yards
(50 grams, 210 meters) per skein]:

Scarf
☐ 2 skeins

Cowl
☐ 2 skeins

Crochet Hook

☐ Size E (3.5 mm) **or** size needed for gauge

Additional Supplies

☐ Tapestry needle (for sewing Cowl)

SIZE INFORMATION

Scarf - 4" wide x 60" long
(10 cm x 152.5 cm)

Cowl - 13½" tall x 40" circumference
(34.5 cm x 101.5 cm)

GAUGE INFORMATION

In pattern,
25 sts and 11 rows = 4" (10 cm)
Gauge Swatch: 4" (10 cm) square
Ch 26.
Rows 1-11: Work same as Scarf,
page 6: 17 sts and 8 ch-1 sps.
Finish off if your project is wider than
4" (10 cm).

INSTRUCTIONS
Scarf

Ch 26.

Row 1 (Right side): Sc in second ch from hook, ★ ch 1, skip next 2 chs, 3 dc in next ch, ch 1, skip next 2 chs, sc in next ch; repeat from ★ across: 17 sts and 8 ch-1 sps.

Note: Loop a short piece of yarn around any stitch to mark Row 1 as **right** side.

Row 2: Ch 3 (**counts as first dc**), turn; dc in first sc, ch 1, skip next dc, sc in next dc, ch 1, ★ skip next dc, (dc, ch 1) twice in next sc, skip next dc, sc in next dc, ch 1; repeat from ★ across to last 2 sts, skip next dc, 2 dc in last sc.

Row 3: Ch 1, turn; sc in first dc, ch 1, skip next dc, 3 dc in next sc, ch 1, ★ skip next ch-1 sp, sc in next ch-1 sp, ch 1, skip next dc, 3 dc in next sc, ch 1; repeat from ★ across to last 2 dc, skip next dc, sc in last dc.

Repeat Rows 2 and 3 for pattern until Scarf measures approximately 60" (152 cm) from beginning ch, ending by working Row 2.

Edging: Ch 1, turn; 2 sc in first dc, sc in next dc and in each dc and ch-1 sp across to last dc, 3 sc in last dc; working in ends of rows, 🎥 sc evenly across to beginning ch; 🎥 working in free loops *(Fig. 3, page 31)* and sps of beginning ch, 3 sc in first ch, 2 sc in next sp, (sc in next ch, 2 sc in next sp) across, 3 sc in ch at base of first sc; working in ends of rows, sc evenly across; sc in same st as first sc; join with slip st to first sc, finish off.

Block Scarf *(see Blocking, page 31)*.

Cowl

Ch 86.

Row 1 (Right side): Sc in second ch from hook, ★ ch 1, skip next 2 chs, 3 dc in next ch, ch 1, skip next 2 chs, sc in next ch; repeat from ★ across: 57 sts and 28 ch-1 sps.

Note: Loop a short piece of yarn around any stitch to mark Row 1 as **right** side.

Row 2: Ch 3 (**counts as first dc**), turn; dc in first sc, ch 1, skip next dc, sc in next dc, ch 1, ★ skip next dc, (dc, ch 1) twice in next sc, skip next dc, sc in next dc, ch 1; repeat from ★ across to last 2 sts, skip next dc, 2 dc in last sc.

Row 3: Ch 1, turn; sc in first dc, ch 1, skip next dc, 3 dc in next sc, ch 1, ★ skip next ch-1 sp, sc in next ch-1 sp, ch 1, skip next dc, 3 dc in next sc, ch 1; repeat from ★ across to last 2 dc, skip next dc, sc in last dc.

Repeat Rows 2 and 3 for pattern until Cowl measures approximately 40" (101.5 cm) from beginning ch, ending by working Row 2.

Finish off leaving a long end for sewing.

Block Cowl *(see Blocking, page 31)*.

With **right** side together, sew short ends of Cowl together. For a Mobius, twist the strip once so that **wrong** and **right** sides are together, then sew short ends together.

CUSTOMIZE YOUR SCARF

The beginning chain for this pattern is a multiple of 6 + 2 *(see Multiples, page 30)*. Choose a size below, work the beginning chain, then follow the instructions until the Scarf measures the desired length. The yarn needed for each size is based on getting the specified gauge with a Super Fine Weight yarn with 230 yards (210 meters) per skein.

Size (inches)	Size (centimeters)	Skein(s) needed	Beginning chain
4 x 40	10 x 101.5	1	26
4 x 54	10 x 137	1	26
4 x 60	10 x 152.5	2	26
6 x 40	15 x 101.5	2	38
6 x 54	15 x 137	2	38
6 x 60	15 x 152.5	2	38
9¾ x 40	25 x 101.5	2	62
9¾ x 54	25 x 137	3	62

CUSTOMIZE YOUR COWL

The beginning chain for this pattern is a multiple of 6 + 2 *(see Multiples, page 30)*. Choose a size below, work the beginning chain, then follow the instructions until the Cowl measures the desired circumference. The yarn needed for each size is based on getting the specified gauge with a Super Fine Weight yarn with 230 yards (210 meters) per skein.

Size (inches)	Size (centimeters)	Skein(s) needed	Beginning chain
4 x 28	10 x 71	1	26
4 x 40	10 x 101.5	1	26
6 x 28	15 x 71	1	38
6 x 40	15 x 101.5	2	38
9¾ x 28	25 x 71	2	62
9¾ x 40	25 x 101.5	2	62
13½ x 28	34.5 x 71	2	86
13½ x 40	34.5 x 101.5	3	86

ANNA

 **EASY**

SIZE INFORMATION

Scarf - 10" wide x 54" long
          (25.5 cm x 137 cm)

Cowl - 5¾" tall x 28" circumference
          (14.5 cm x 71 cm)

GAUGE INFORMATION

In pattern,
    11 sts and 8 rows = 3¾" (9.5 cm)
Gauge Swatch: 3¾" (9.5 cm) square
Ch 13.
Rows 1-8: Work same as Scarf,
page 10: 11 sts.
Finish off if your project is wider than
3¾" (9.5 cm).

INSTRUCTIONS
Scarf

Ch 31.

Row 1 (Right side)**:** Hdc in third ch from hook **(2 skipped chs count as first hdc)**, ★ skip next ch, (sc, hdc) in next ch; repeat from ★ across to last 2 chs, skip next ch, sc in last ch: 29 sts.

Note: Loop a short piece of yarn around any stitch to mark Row 1 as **right** side.

Row 2: Ch 2 **(counts as first hdc)**, turn; hdc in first sc, ★ skip next hdc, (sc, hdc) in next sc; repeat from ★ across to last 2 hdc, skip next hdc, sc in last hdc.

Repeat Row 2 for pattern until Scarf measures approximately 54" (137 cm) from beginning ch.

Finish off.

Block Scarf *(see Blocking, page 31)*.

Cowl

Ch 19.

Row 1 (Right side)**:** Hdc in third ch from hook **(2 skipped chs count as first hdc)**, ★ skip next ch, (sc, hdc) in next ch; repeat from ★ across to last 2 chs, skip next ch, sc in last ch: 17 sts.

Note: Loop a short piece of yarn around any stitch to mark Row 1 as **right** side.

Row 2: Ch 2 **(counts as first hdc)**, turn; hdc in first sc, ★ skip next hdc, (sc, hdc) in next sc; repeat from ★ across to last 2 hdc, skip next hdc, sc in last hdc.

Repeat Row 2 for pattern until Cowl measures approximately 28" (71 cm) from beginning ch, ending by working a **wrong** side row.

Finish off leaving a long end for sewing.

Block Cowl *(see Blocking, page 31)*.

With **right** side together, sew short ends of Cowl together. For a Mobius, twist the strip once so that **wrong** and **right** sides are together, then sew short ends together.

CUSTOMIZE YOUR SCARF

The beginning chain for this pattern is a multiple of
2 + 1 *(see Multiples, page 30)*. Choose a size below,
work the beginning chain, then follow the instructions
until the Scarf measures the desired length. The yarn
needed for each size is based on getting the specified
gauge with a Medium Weight yarn with 147 yards
(135 meters) per skein.

Size (inches)	Size (centimeters)	Skein(s) needed	Beginning chain
3¾ x 40	9.5 x 101.5	1	13
3¾ x 54	9.5 x 137	2	13
3¾ x 60	9.5 x 152.5	2	13
5¾ x 40	14.5 x 101.5	2	19
5¾ x 54	14.5 x 137	2	19
5¾ x 60	14.5 x 152.5	2	19
10 x 40	25.5 x 101.5	3	31
10 x 54	25.5 x 137	3	31

CUSTOMIZE YOUR COWL

The beginning chain for this pattern is a multiple of
2 + 1 *(see Multiples, page 30)*. Choose a size below,
work the beginning chain, then follow the instructions
until the Cowl measures the desired circumference.
The yarn needed for each size is based on getting
the specified gauge with a Medium Weight yarn with
147 yards (135 meters) per skein.

Size (inches)	Size (centimeters)	Skein(s) needed	Beginning chain
3¾ x 28	9.5 x 71	1	13
3¾ x 40	9.5 x 101.5	1	13
5¾ x 28	14.5 x 71	1	19
5¾ x 40	14.5 x 101.5	2	19
10 x 28	25.5 x 71	2	31
10 x 40	25.5 x 101.5	3	31
12 x 28	30.5 x 71	2	37
12 x 40	30.5 x 101.5	3	37

BESSIE

 **EASY**

SIZE INFORMATION

Scarf - 6" wide x 59¾" long

(15 cm x 152 cm)

Cowl - 9½" tall x 28½" circumference

(24 cm x 72.5 cm)

GAUGE INFORMATION

In pattern, 19 sts = 5" (12.75 cm);

8 rows = 4" (10 cm)

Gauge Swatch: 5" wide x 4" high

(12.75 cm x 10 cm)

Ch 24.

Rows 1-8: Work same as Scarf, page 14:

16 dc and 4 ch-1 sps.

Finish off.

Each row of the Scarf or the Cowl is worked across the length of the piece.

INSTRUCTIONS
Scarf

Ch 232.

Row 1 (Right side): Working in back ridge of beginning ch *(Fig. 1, page 30)*, 3 dc in eighth ch from hook **(first 4 skipped chs count as first dc plus ch 1)**, ch 1, ★ skip next 3 chs, 3 dc in next ch, ch 1; repeat from ★ across to last 4 chs, skip next 3 chs, dc in last ch: 170 dc and 57 ch-1 sps.

Note: Loop a short piece of yarn around any stitch to mark Row 1 as **right** side.

Row 2: Ch 3 **(counts as first dc)**, turn; 2 dc in next ch-1 sp, (ch 1, 3 dc in next ch-1 sp) across to last dc, dc in last dc: 172 dc and 56 ch-1 sps.

Row 3: Ch 4 **(counts as first dc plus ch 1)**, turn; (3 dc in next ch-1 sp, ch 1) across to last 3 dc, skip next 2 dc, dc in last dc: 170 dc and 57 ch-1 sps.

Rows 4-12: Repeat Rows 2 and 3, 4 times; then repeat Row 2 once **more**: 172 dc and 56 ch-1 sps.

Trim: Ch 1, turn; sc evenly around working 3 sc in each corner; join with slip st to first sc, finish off.

Block Scarf *(see Blocking, page 31)*.

Cowl

Ch 112.

Row 1 (Right side): Working in back ridge of beginning ch *(Fig. 1, page 30)*, 3 dc in eighth ch from hook **(first 4 skipped chs count as first dc plus ch 1)**, ch 1, ★ skip next 3 chs, 3 dc in next ch, ch 1; repeat from ★ across to last 4 chs, skip next 3 chs, dc in last ch: 80 dc and 27 ch-1 sps.

Note: Loop a short piece of yarn around any stitch to mark Row 1 as **right** side.

Row 2: Ch 3 **(counts as first dc)**, turn; 2 dc in next ch-1 sp, (ch 1, 3 dc in next ch-1 sp) across to last dc, dc in last dc: 82 dc and 26 ch-1 sps.

Row 3: Ch 4 **(counts as first dc plus ch 1)**, turn; (3 dc in next ch-1 sp, ch 1) across to last 3 dc, skip next 2 dc, dc in last dc: 80 dc and 27 ch-1 sps.

Rows 4-19: Repeat Rows 2 and 3, 8 times: 80 dc and 27 ch-1 sps.

Finish off leaving a long end for sewing.

Block Cowl *(see Blocking, page 31)*.

With **right** side together, sew short ends of Cowl together. For a Mobius, twist the strip once so that **wrong** and **right** sides are together, then sew short ends together.

CUSTOMIZE YOUR SCARF

The beginning chain for this pattern is a multiple of 4 *(see Multiples, page 31)*. Choose a size below, work the beginning chain, then follow the instructions until the Scarf measures the desired width. The yarn needed for each size is based on getting the specified gauge with a Medium Weight yarn with 279 yards (256 meters) per skein.

Size (inches)	Size (centimeters)	Skein(s) needed	Beginning chain
4 x 42	10 x 106.5	1	164
4 x 53½	10 x 136	1	208
4 x 59¾	10 x 152	1	232
6 x 42	15 x 106.5	1	164
6 x 53½	15 x 136	2	208
6 x 59¾	15 x 152	2	232
9½ x 42	24 x 106.5	2	164
9½ x 53½	24 x 136	2	208

CUSTOMIZE YOUR COWL

The beginning chain for this pattern is a multiple of 4 *(see Multiples, page 31)*. Choose a size below, work the beginning chain, then follow the instructions until the Cowl measures the desired height. The yarn needed for each size is based on getting the specified gauge with a Medium Weight yarn with 279 yards (256 meters) per skein.

Size (inches)	Size (centimeters)	Skein(s) needed	Beginning chain
4 x 28½	10 x 72.5	1	112
4 x 42	10 x 106.5	1	164
6 x 28½	15 x 72.5	1	112
6 x 42	15 x 106.5	1	164
9½ x 28½	24 x 72.5	1	112
9½ x 42	24 x 106.5	2	164
12 x 28½	30.5 x 72.5	2	112
12 x 42	30.5 x 106.5	2	164

MARIA

 EASY

SHOPPING LIST

Yarn (Bulky Weight)

[3 ounces, 90 yards
(85 grams, 81 meters) per skein]:

Scarf

☐ 4 skeins

Cowl

☐ 2 skeins

Crochet Hook

☐ Size K (6.5 mm) **or** size needed for gauge

Additional Supplies

☐ Yarn needle (for sewing Cowl)

SIZE INFORMATION

Scarf - 12" wide x 54" long
    (30.5 cm x 137 cm)

Cowl - 5" tall x 54" circumference
    (12.5 cm x 137 cm)

GAUGE INFORMATION

In pattern,

    13 sts and 8 rows = 5" (12.75 cm)

Gauge Swatch: 5" (12.75 cm) square

Rows 1-8: Work same as Cowl,
page 18: 8 sts and 3 sps.

Finish off if your project is wider than
5" (12.5 cm).

——— STITCH GUIDE ———

 FOUNDATION SINGLE
    CROCHET (abbreviated fsc)

Ch 2, insert hook in second ch from
hook, YO and pull up a loop, YO and
draw through one loop on hook
(**ch made**), YO and draw through
both loops on hook (**first fsc made**),
★ insert hook in ch at base of last
fsc made, YO and pull up a loop, YO
and draw through one loop on hook
(**ch made**), YO and draw through both
loops on hook (**fsc made**); repeat
from ★ for each additional st.

INSTRUCTIONS
Scarf

Row 1 (Right side): Work 31 fsc.

Note: Loop a short piece of yarn around any stitch to mark Row 1 as **right** side.

Row 2: Ch 1, turn; sc in first 2 fsc, ch 5, ★ skip next 3 fsc, sc in next 3 fsc, ch 5; repeat from ★ across to last 5 fsc, skip next 3 fsc, sc in last 2 fsc: 16 sc and 5 ch-5 sps.

Row 3: Ch 3 (**counts as first dc**), turn; dc in next sc, ch 1, sc in next ch-5 sp, ch 1, ★ dc in next 3 sc, ch 1, sc in next ch-5 sp, ch 1; repeat from ★ across to last 2 sc, dc in last 2 sc: 21 sts and 10 ch-1 sps.

Row 4: Ch 5 (**counts as first dc plus ch 2**), turn; skip next dc, sc in next ch-1 sp and in next sc, sc in next ch-1 sp, ★ ch 5, skip next 3 dc, sc in next ch-1 sp and in next sc, sc in next ch-1 sp; repeat from ★ across to last 2 dc, ch 2, skip next dc, dc in last dc: 17 sts and 6 sps.

Row 5: Ch 1, turn; sc in first dc, ch 1, dc in next 3 sc, ch 1, ★ sc in next ch-5 sp, ch 1, dc in next 3 sc, ch 1; repeat from ★ across to next ch-2 sp, skip next ch-2 sp, sc in last dc: 21 sts and 10 ch-1 sps.

Row 6: Ch 1, turn; sc in first sc and in next ch-1 sp, ch 5, skip next 3 dc, sc in next ch-1 sp and in next sc, ★ sc in next ch-1 sp, ch 5, skip next 3 dc, sc in next ch-1 sp and in next sc; repeat from ★ across: 16 sc and 5 ch-5 sps.

Repeat Rows 3-6 for pattern until Scarf measures approximately 54" (137 cm) from beginning ch, ending by working Row 5.

Finish off.

Block Scarf *(see Blocking, page 31).*

Cowl

Follow Scarf Instructions for Cowls wider than 5" (12.5 cm).

Row 1 (Right side): Work 13 fsc.

Note: Loop a short piece of yarn around any stitch to mark Row 1 as **right** side.

Row 2: Ch 1, turn; sc in first 2 fsc, ch 5, skip next 3 fsc, sc in next 3 fsc, ch 5, skip next 3 fsc, sc in last 2 fsc: 7 sc and 2 ch-5 sps.

Row 3: Ch 3 (**counts as first dc**), turn; dc in next sc, ch 1, sc in next ch-5 sp, ch 1, dc in next 3 sc, ch 1, sc in next ch-5 sp, ch 1, dc in last 2 sc: 9 sts and 4 ch-1 sps.

Row 4: Ch 5 (**counts as first dc plus ch 2**), turn; † sc in next ch-1 sp and in next sc, sc in next ch-1 sp †, ch 5, skip next 3 dc, repeat from † to † once, ch 2, skip next dc, dc in last dc: 8 sts and 3 sps.

Row 5: Ch 1, turn; sc in first dc, ch 1, dc in next 3 sc, ch 1, sc in next ch-5 sp, ch 1, dc in next 3 sc, ch 1, sc in last dc: 9 sts and 4 ch-1 sps.

Row 6: Ch 1, turn; sc in first sc and in next ch-1 sp, † ch 5, skip next 3 dc, sc in next ch-1 sp and in next sc †, sc in next ch-1 sp, repeat from † to † once: 7 sc and 2 ch-5 sps.

Repeat Rows 3-6 for pattern until Cowl measures approximately 54" (137 cm) from beginning edge, ending by working Row 5.

Finish off leaving a long end for sewing.

Block Cowl *(see Blocking, page 31).* With **right** side together, sew short ends of Cowl together. For a Mobius, twist the strip once so that **wrong** and **right** sides are together, then sew short ends together.

CUSTOMIZE YOUR SCARF

The foundation single crochets for this pattern are a multiple of 6 + 1 *(see Multiples, page 30)*. Choose a size below, work the required number of foundation single crochets, then follow the instructions until the Scarf measures the desired length. The yarn needed for each size is based on getting the specified gauge with a Bulky Weight yarn with 90 yards (81 meters) per skein.

Size (inches)	Size (centimeters)	Skein(s) needed	Fsc needed
5 x 40	12.5 x 101.5	2	13
5 x 54	12.5 x 137	2	13
5 x 60	12.5 x 152.5	2	13
7¼ x 40	18.5 x 101.5	2	19
7¼ x 54	18.5 x 137	2	19
7¼ x 60	18.5 x 152.5	3	19
9½ x 40	24 x 101.5	2	25
9½ x 54	24 x 137	3	25

CUSTOMIZE YOUR COWL

The foundation single crochets for this pattern are a multiple of 6 + 1 *(see Multiples, page 30)*. Choose a size below, work the required number of foundation single crochets, then follow the instructions until the Cowl measures the desired circumference. The yarn needed for each size is based on getting the specified gauge with a Bulky Weight yarn with 90 yards (81 meters) per skein.

Size (inches)	Size (centimeters)	Skein(s) needed	Fsc needed
5 x 28	12.5 x 71	1	13
5 x 40	12.5 x 101.5	2	13
7¼ x 28	18.5 x 71	2	19
7¼ x 40	18.5 x 101.5	2	19
9½ x 28	24 x 71	2	25
9½ x 40	24 x 101.5	2	25
12 x 28	30.5 x 71	2	31
12 x 40	30.5 x 101.5	3	31

MARTHA

 **EASY**

SIZE INFORMATION

Scarf - 6" wide x 60½" long
           (15 cm x 153.5 cm)

Cowl - 4" tall x 44" circumference
           (10 cm x 112 cm)

GAUGE INFORMATION

In pattern,
    one repeat (17 sts) = 5½" (14 cm);
    8 rows = 4" (10 cm)

Gauge Swatch: 11" wide x 4" tall
    (28 cm x 10 cm)

Ch 37.

Rows 1-8: Work same as Scarf,
page 22: 34 sc.

Finish off.

Each row of the Scarf or the Cowl is
worked across the length of the piece.

INSTRUCTIONS
Scarf
Ch 190.

Row 1 (Right side): Working in back ridge of beginning ch (*Fig. 1, page 30*), dc in fourth ch from hook **(3 skipped chs count as first dc)**, 2 dc in each of next 2 chs, (skip next ch, dc in next ch) 5 times, ★ skip next ch, 2 dc in each of next 6 chs, (skip next ch, dc in next ch) 5 times; repeat from ★ across to last 4 chs, skip next ch, 2 dc in each of last 3 chs: 187 dc.

Note: Loop a short piece of yarn around any stitch to mark Row 1 as **right** side.

Row 2: Ch 1, turn; sc in first dc and in each dc across.

Row 3: Ch 3 **(counts as first dc)**, turn; working in Back Loops Only (*Fig. 2, page 30)*, dc in first sc, 2 dc in each of next 2 sc, (skip next sc, dc in next sc) 5 times, ★ skip next sc, 2 dc in each of next 6 sc, (skip next sc, dc in next sc) 5 times; repeat from ★ across to last 4 sc, skip next sc, 2 dc in each of last 3 sc.

Rows 4-12: Repeat Rows 2 and 3, 4 times; then repeat Row 2 once **more.**

Finish off.

Block Scarf *(see Blocking, page 31)*.

Cowl
Ch 139.

Row 1 (Right side): Working in back ridge of beginning ch (*Fig. 1, page 30)*, dc in fourth ch from hook **(3 skipped chs count as first dc)**, 2 dc in each of next 2 chs, (skip next ch, dc in next ch) 5 times, ★ skip next ch, 2 dc in each of next 6 chs, (skip next ch, dc in next ch) 5 times; repeat from ★ across to last 4 chs, skip next ch, 2 dc in each of last 3 chs: 136 dc.

Note: Loop a short piece of yarn around any stitch to mark Row 1 as **right** side.

Row 2: Ch 1, turn; sc in same st and in each dc across.

Row 3: Ch 3 **(counts as first dc)**, turn; working in Back Loops Only (*Fig. 2, page 30)*, dc in first sc, 2 dc in each of next 2 sc, (skip next sc, dc in next sc) 5 times, ★ skip next sc, 2 dc in each of next 6 sc, (skip next sc, dc in next sc) 5 times; repeat from ★ across to last 4 sc, skip next sc, 2 dc in each of last 3 sc.

Rows 4-8: Repeat Rows 2 and 3 twice; then repeat Row 2 once **more.**

Finish off leaving a long end for sewing.

Block Cowl *(see Blocking, page 31)*.

With **right** side together, sew short ends of Cowl together.

CUSTOMIZE YOUR SCARF

The beginning chain for this pattern is a multiple of 17 + 3 *(see Multiples, page 30)*. Chose a size below, work the beginning chain, then follow the instructions until the Scarf measures the desired width. The yarn needed for each size is based on getting the specified gauge with a Medium Weight yarn with 153 yards (140 meters) per skein.

Size (inches)	Size (centimeters)	Skein(s) needed	Beginning chain
5 x 38½	12.5 x 98	1	122
5 x 44	12.5 x 112	2	139
5 x 60½	12.5 x 153.5	2	190
6 x 38½	15 x 98	2	122
6 x 44	15 x 112	2	139
6 x 60½	15 x 153.5	2	190
10 x 38½	25.5 x 98	2	122
10 x 44	25.5 x 112	3	139

CUSTOMIZE YOUR COWL

The beginning chain for this pattern is a multiple of 17 + 3 *(see Multiples, page 30)*. Chose a size below, work the beginning chain, then follow the instructions the Cowl measures the desired height. The yarn needed for each size is based on getting the specified gauge with a Medium Weight yarn with 153 yards (140 meters) per skein.

Size (inches)	Size (centimeters)	Skein(s) needed	Beginning chain
5 x 27½	12.5 x 70	1	88
5 x 38½	12.5 x 98	1	122
6 x 27½	15 x 70	1	88
6 x 38½	15 x 98	2	122
10 x 27½	25.5 x 70	2	88
10 x 38½	25.5 x 98	2	122
12 x 27½	30.5 x 70	2	88
12 x 38½	30.5 x 98	3	122

DIANE

 **EASY**

SHOPPING LIST

Yarn (Medium Weight)
[3 ounces, 252 yards
(85 grams, 230 meters) per skein]:

Scarf
☐ 1 skein

Cowl
☐ 1 skein

Crochet Hook
☐ Size H (5 mm) **or** size needed for gauge

Additional Supplies
☐ Yarn needle (for sewing Cowl)

SIZE INFORMATION

Scarf - 3" wide x 53½" long
(7.5 cm x 136 cm)

Cowl - 4¾" tall x 39½" circumference
(12 cm x 100.5 cm)

GAUGE INFORMATION

In pattern, (Cross St, ch 1) 5 times
(20 sts) = 5" (12.5 cm);
Rows 1-10 = 3¾" (9.5 cm)

Gauge Swatch: 5½" x 3¾"
(14 cm x 9.5 cm)

Row 1: Work 23 fsc.

Rows 2-10: Work same as Cowl,
page 27: 5 Cross Sts.
Finish off.

Each row of the Scarf or the Cowl is
worked across the length of the piece.
Chains are counted as stitches.

ENDING CROSS ST DECREASE

(uses last 4 sts)

Skip next 3 sts, dc in last sc, ch 1, working **around** dc just made, YO, insert hook in second skipped st, YO and pull up a loop, YO and draw through 2 loops on hook, [YO, insert hook in **same** sc as last dc made, YO and pull up a loop, YO and draw through 2 loops on hook, YO and draw through all 3 loops on hook **(counts as last dc of Cross St)]**.

INSTRUCTIONS
Scarf

Row 1 (Right side)**:** Work 215 fsc.

Note: Loop a short piece of yarn around any stitch to mark Row 1 as **right** side.

Row 2: Ch 4 **(counts as first dc plus ch 1, now and throughout)**, turn; (work Cross St, ch 1) across to last 2 fsc, skip next fsc, dc in last fsc: 53 Cross Sts.

Row 3: Ch 1, turn; sc in first dc, (ch 1, sc in next dc) across: 215 sts.

Row 4: Ch 2, turn; work beginning Cross St decrease, ch 1, (work Cross St, ch 1) across to last 4 sts, work ending Cross St decrease: 54 Cross Sts.

Row 5: Ch 1, turn; sc in first dc, (ch 1, sc in next dc) across: 215 sts.

───── STITCH GUIDE ─────

FOUNDATION SINGLE CROCHET *(abbreviated fsc)*

Ch 2, insert hook in second ch from hook, YO and pull up a loop, YO and draw through one loop on hook **(ch made)**, YO and draw through both loops on hook **(first fsc made)**, ★ insert hook in ch at base of last fsc made, YO and pull up a loop, YO and draw through one loop on hook **(ch made)**, YO and draw through both loops on hook **(fsc made)**; repeat from ★ for each additional st.

CROSS STITCH

(abbreviated Cross St) (uses 4 sts)

Skip next 3 sts, dc in next st, ch 1, working **around** dc just made, dc in second skipped st.

BEGINNING CROSS ST DECREASE

(uses first 3 sts)

Skip next ch, dc in next sc, ch 1, working **around** dc just made, dc in **same** st as turning ch-2.

Row 6: Ch 4, turn; (work Cross St, ch 1) across to last 2 sts, skip next ch, dc in last sc: 53 Cross Sts.

Rows 7-9: Repeat Rows 3-5.

Finish off.

Block Scarf *(see Blocking, page 31).*

Cowl

Row 1 (Right side)**:** Work 159 fsc.

Note: Loop a short piece of yarn around any stitch to mark Row 1 as **right** side.

Row 2: Ch 4 (**counts as first dc plus ch 1, now and throughout**), turn; (work Cross St, ch 1) across to last 2 fsc, skip next fsc, dc in last fsc: 39 Cross Sts.

Row 3: Ch 1, turn; sc in first dc, (ch 1, sc in next dc) across: 159 sts.

Row 4: Ch 2, turn; work beginning Cross St decrease, ch 1, (work Cross St, ch 1) across to last 4 sts, work ending Cross St decrease: 40 Cross Sts.

Row 5: Ch 1, turn; sc in first dc, (ch 1, sc in next dc) across: 159 sts.

Row 6: Ch 4, turn; (work Cross St, ch 1) across to last 2 sts, skip next ch, dc in last sc: 39 Cross Sts.

Rows 7-13: Repeat Rows 3-6 once, then repeat Rows 3-5 once **more**; finish off leaving a long end for sewing.

Block Cowl *(see Blocking, page 31).*

With **right** side together, sew short ends of Cowl together. For a Mobius, twist the strip once so that **wrong** and **right** sides are together, then sew short ends together.

CUSTOMIZE YOUR SCARF

The foundation single crochets for this pattern are a multiple of 4 + 3 *(see Multiples, page 30)*. Choose a size below, work Row 1 with the required number of foundation single crochets, then follow the instructions until the Scarf measures the desired width. The yarn needed for each size is based on getting the specified gauge with a Medium Weight yarn with 252 yards (230 meters) per skein.

Size (inches)	Size (centimeters)	Skein(s) needed	Fsc needed
3 x 39½	7.5 x 99	1	159
3 x 53½	7.5 x 136	1	215
3 x 59½	7.5 x 151	1	239
6 x 39½	15 x 99	1	159
6 x 53½	15 x 136	2	215
6 x 59½	15 x 151	2	239
10 x 39½	25.5 x 99	2	159
10 x 53½	25.5 x 136	2	215

CUSTOMIZE YOUR COWL

The foundation single crochets for this pattern are a multiple of 4 + 3 *(see Multiples, page 30)*. Choose a size below, work Row 1 with the required number of foundation single crochets, then follow the instructions until the Cowl measures the desired height. The yarn needed for each size is based on getting the specified gauge with a Medium Weight yarn with 252 yards (230 meters) per skein.

Size (inches)	Size (centimeters)	Skein(s) needed	Fsc needed
3 x 27½	7.5 x 70	1	111
3 x 39½	7.5 x 99	1	159
6 x 27½	15 x 70	1	111
6 x 39½	15 x 99	1	159
10 x 27½	25.5 x 70	1	111
10 x 39½	25.5 x 99	2	159
12 x 27½	30.5 x 70	2	111
12 x 39½	30.5 x 99	2	159

GENERAL INSTRUCTIONS

ABBREVIATIONS

ch(s)	chain(s)
cm	centimeters
dc	double crochet(s)
fsc	foundation single crochet(s)
hdc	half double crochet(s)
mm	millimeters
sc	single crochet(s)
sp(s)	space(s)
st(s)	stitch(es)
YO	yarn over

SYMBOLS & TERMS

★ — work instructions following ★ as many **more** times as indicated in addition to the first time.

† to † — work all of the instructions from first † to second † **as many** times as specified.

( ) or [ ] — work enclosed instructions **as many** times as specified by the number immediately following **or** work all enclosed instructions in the stitch or space indicated **or** contains explanatory remarks.

colon (:) — the number(s) given after a colon at the end of a row denote(s) the number of stitches you should have on that row.

CROCHET TERMINOLOGY		
UNITED STATES		**INTERNATIONAL**
slip stitch (slip st)	=	single crochet (sc)
single crochet (sc)	=	double crochet (dc)
half double crochet (hdc)	=	half treble crochet (htr)
double crochet (dc)	=	treble crochet(tr)
treble crochet (tr)	=	double treble crochet (dtr)
double treble crochet (dtr)	=	triple treble crochet (ttr)
triple treble crochet (tr tr)	=	quadruple treble crochet (qtr)
skip	=	miss

GAUGE

Exact gauge is **essential** for proper size. Before beginning your project, make the sample swatch given in the individual instructions in the yarn and hook specified. After completing the swatch, measure it, counting your stitches and rows carefully. If your swatch is larger or smaller than specified, **make another, changing hook size to get the correct gauge.** Keep trying until you find the size hook that will give you the specified gauge.

Yarn Weight Symbol & Names	LACE 0	SUPER FINE 1	FINE 2	LIGHT 3	MEDIUM 4	BULKY 5	SUPER BULKY 6
Type of Yarns in Category	Fingering, 10-count crochet thread	Sock, Fingering Baby	Sport, Baby	DK, Light Worsted	Worsted, Afghan, Aran	Chunky, Craft, Rug	Bulky, Roving
Crochet Gauge* Ranges in Single Crochet to 4" (10 cm)	32-42 double crochets**	21-32 sts	16-20 sts	12-17 sts	11-14 sts	8-11 sts	5-9 sts
Advised Hook Size Range	Steel*** 6,7,8 Regular hook B-1	B-1 to E-4	E-4 to 7	7 to I-9	I-9 to K-10.5	K-10.5 to M-13	M-13 and larger

*GUIDELINES ONLY: The chart above reflects the most commonly used gauges and hook sizes for specific yarn categories.

** Lace weight yarns are usually crocheted on larger-size hooks to create lacy openwork patterns. Accordingly, a gauge range is difficult to determine. Always follow the gauge stated in your pattern.

*** Steel crochet hooks are sized differently from regular hooks–the higher the number the smaller the hook, which is the reverse of regular hook sizing.

CROCHET HOOKS																	
U.S.	B-1	C-2	D-3	E-4	F-5	G-6	7	H-8	I-9	J-10	K-10½	L-11	M/N-13	N/P-15	P/Q	Q	S
Metric - mm	2.25	2.75	3.25	3.5	3.75	4	4.5	5	5.5	6	6.5	8	9	10	15	16	19

■□□□ BEGINNER	Projects for first-time crocheters using basic stitches. Minimal shaping.
■■□□ EASY	Projects using yarn with basic stitches, repetitive stitch patterns, simple color changes, and simple shaping and finishing.
■■■□ INTERMEDIATE	Projects using a variety of techniques, such as basic lace patterns or color patterns, mid-level shaping and finishing.
■■■■ EXPERIENCED	Projects with intricate stitch patterns, techniques and dimension, such as non-repeating patterns, multi-color techniques, fine threads, small hooks, detailed shaping and refined finishing.

MULTIPLES

Multiples indicate the number of chains required to form one full repeat of a pattern. We have provided the math for many variations of each pattern in the Customize Your Scarf/Cowl charts. If you wish to branch out to make narrower/wider or shorter/longer versions than the ones found in the charts, do not hesitate to add or subtract chains in order for your beginning chain to correspond with the multiple for your chosen pattern. To allow the pattern to work across the beginning chain, make sure to add the number (if any) after the multiple to your chain. Multiples also apply to the foundation single crochets in Maria, page 16 and Diane, page 24. Begin those projects with the multiple of the foundation single crochets indicated plus any additional stitches to have the right number.

Example: Multiple of 17 + 3 means that you need 17 chains for each repeat of the pattern plus an extra 3 chains.

If you wish to repeat the pattern twice, you would chain 37, 2 repeats of 17 is 34 plus 3 extra chains = 37 chains; 3 repeats would require 54 chains (3 repeats of 17 = 51 plus 3 extra chains = 54 chains) and so on.

Gauge **does** have an impact on the size of your project; in order for your Scarf or Cowl to be the size you want, you need to match the gauge given *(see Gauge, page 29)*.

BACK RIDGE

Work only in loop(s) indicated by arrows *(Fig. 1)*.

Fig. 1

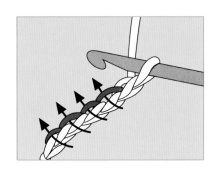

BACK LOOPS ONLY

Work only in loop(s) indicated by arrows *(Fig. 2)*.

Fig. 2

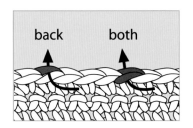

back   both

FREE LOOPS OF A CHAIN

When instructed to work in free loops of a chain, work in loop indicated by arrow *(Fig. 3)*.

Fig. 3

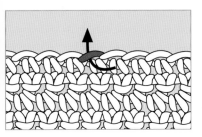

BLOCKING

Blocking helps to smooth your work and give it a professional appearance. Check the yarn label for any special instructions about blocking.

With acrylics that can be blocked, place your project on a clean terry towel over a flat surface and pin it in place to the desired size using rust-proof pins where needed. Cover it with dampened bath towels. When the towels are dry, the project is blocked.

If the yarn is hand washable, carefully launder your project using a mild soap or detergent, being careful to gently squeeze suds through the piece. Rinse it several times in cool, clear water without wringing or twisting. Remove any excess moisture by rolling it in a succession of dry terry towels. You can put it in the final spin cycle of your washer, without water. Lay the project on a large towel on a flat surface out of direct sunlight. Gently smooth and pat it to the desired size and shape. When it is completely dry, it is blocked.

Another method of blocking that is especially good for wool requires a steam iron or a hand-held steamer. Place your project on a clean terry towel over a flat surface and shape; pin it in place using rust-proof pins where needed. Hold a steam iron or steamer just above the item and steam it thoroughly. Never let the weight of the iron touch the item because it will flatten the stitches. Leave the item pinned until it is completely dry.

YARN INFORMATION

Projects in this book were made using a variety of yarn weights. Any brand of the specified weight of yarn may be used. It is best to refer to the yardage/meters when determining how many balls or skeins to purchase. Remember, to arrive at the finished size, it is the GAUGE/TENSION that is important, not the brand of yarn.

For your convenience, listed below are the specific colors used to create our photography models.

MARY
Premier Yarn® Deborah Norville Collection™ Serenity™ Sock
Scarf - #0808 Aquamarine
Premier Yarn® Deborah Norville Collection™ Serenity™ Sock Solids
Cowl - #5007 Woodsy Green

ANNA
Lion Brand® Amazing®
Scarf - #208 Glacier Bay
Cowl - #206 Arcadia

BESSIE
Red Heart® Boutique Unforgettable™
Scarf - #3940 Echo
Cowl - #3960 Tidal

MARIA
Patons® ColorWul™
Scarf - #90425 Jardin
Cowl - #90521 Countryside

MARTHA
Red Heart® Boutique Midnight®
Scarf - #1945 Shadow
Cowl - #9803 Borealis

DIANE
Patons® Metallic™
Scarf - #95134 Blue Steel
Cowl - #95420 Burnished Rose Gold

Production Team: Writer/Instructional Editor - Sarah J. Green; Editorial Writer - Susan Frantz Wiles; Senior Graphic Artist - Lora Puls; Graphic Artist - Jacqueline Breazeal; Photo Stylist - Lori Wenger; and Photographer - Jason Masters.